THE RING MASTER PLAN

Single Women's Guide to Becoming a Wife

Brent & Angel Rhodes

Cover Design:

Email requests to: info@MarriageofGod.com

Ordering Information:
Quantity sales. Special discounts are available on quantity purchases by corporations, associations, and others. For details, contact the publisher at the email address above.
Orders by U.S. trade bookstores and wholesalers. Please contact Publisher
Tel: (843) 832-1119 or visit www.MarriageofGod.com.

Published by: Brent & Angel Rhodes

Printed in the United States of America

First Edition: 2017

ISBN 978-0999099001

Dedication

We dedicate this book to our mothers,
Theresa R. Jones & Martha L. Rhodes

Thank you and we love you!

TABLE OF CONTENTS

INTRODUCTION

Since 2010, the anthem to all women in relationships has been Beyonce's "Single Ladies". The anthem is encouraging men to put a ring on it. With the song going over quadruple-platinum in sales and winning 3 Grammy Awards, the single ladies voices were heard loud and clear. With your voice being heard it has to be clear and concise. You have to explain what you want and understand what you do not want. If you want The Ring, you must understand what it takes to get The Ring. Please don't accept the ring from just anyone.

This book will unveil the dynamics of The Ring that every woman should know. After reading this book, you will be prepared to know when to say yes and when to say no. This book will answer questions and explain concepts about The Ring that the song and even conversations with your girlfriends are unable to adequately address. It has been said that timing is everything. Single ladies often question the expected time line for their relationships. This book will explain a timeline of actions, not merely dates. Receiving The Ring is the event before the Big Event and this book will explain the significance of The Ring.

Having been coaches, advisors and relationship mentors for close to two decades now, we have encountered countless single ladies wondering what they should expect as a bride-to-be. After helping hundreds of women with their relationships, we found that they all had similar questions. So, we decided to write The Ring Master Plan to answer those questions and to help the women who may not be able to contact us.

We have seen many of our clients, go from not being in relationships and doubting that they would ever love again, to now being engaged and in love after learning the principles to being in position. We have also helped thousands of marriages by teaching them principles they wish they had known before they said I do. It is now our God-given purpose to help prepare single women to become wives.

The Ring Master Plan will help you to determine if you are really concerned about being engaged to be married or if you just want a man to give you a ring. In this book, we also give help you to determine if he's just providing a ring to shut you up. The Ring Master Plan will explain to you when should say no to the ring.

If you are in a relationship, you deserve The Ring and nothing less, but NOT by any means necessary. We challenge you to read this book with and open mind and an open heart. This way you will learn the true meaning of being in position of being found. The Ring Master Plan is not for those who want to compromise their self-worth. It is for those who realize that they are the prize!

CHAPTER 1

Do You Really Want the Ring?

"This is the confidence we have in approaching God: that if we ask anything according to his will, he hears us." 1 John 5:14

L ife is a journey. It will have its ups and it has its downs. There will be many trials and tribulations, but it wouldn't be real life if you didn't have these things! Of all the things that you will experience in life, love is one of the most important. Whether it is the love between parent and child, or the romantic love between a man and women that can lead to marriage, love is undoubtedly one of the greatest pleasures in this life. It is this romantic love in the marital aspect that we'll be focusing on.

Marriage, in and of itself, is also one of the most important experiences that this life holds. It will undoubtedly have some tough times and bring some "realities" to your doorstep. We know that these realities will appear in the form of some very challenging at times. It doesn't matter if you've been married for years, if you're newlyweds, a pre-marital couple, or if you are single; if you're willing to do things God's way, then He will see that you will make it through any storm! With that being said, we'd like to talk to the singles for a while. You have to ask yourself a very important question:

Do you really want the ring?

When you enter into relationships, marriage is the expectation these days. Beyonce' has a song specifically addressing the single ladies! We are not saying that there's anything wrong with expecting marriage from a relationship. In fact, marriage *should* be the expected end result!

However, what happens far too often is that you get into relationships without having a clear understanding of what you want. You may tell yourself what you want and honestly believe it to be true. Then when you actually get it, you realize that it's the exact *opposite* of what your heart truly desires.

"What in the world have I gotten myself into?"

That's the question you may end up asking yourself when you find yourself stuck in those wrong relationships. If this describes you are currently, or has ever been you at some point in time, you need to ask yourself some tough questions. You don't have to tell anybody else the answer to these questions. However, as Polonius said in Hamlet "To thine own self be true." So, dig deep, look inwardly and answer honestly. This is your season of singleness, and your *Season of Singleness* is all about two things; preparation and restoration! Marriage takes preparation! And if you're newly single, then you need to go through the process of restoration in order to be ready for that commitment!

Many single ladies want the ring, but they don't realize that there is a cost associated with that ring, and we're not just talking about a monetary value! You have to be fully prepared, because a marriage is work! In order for you to be ready to receive that ring, you must first be willing to work on yourself.

We often say that a wedding is an expensive conversation, but a marriage is a *brilliant* investment. To the women reading this, we are sure that even at a very young age you have had dreams of you on your

> **'A wedding is an expensive conversation, but a marriage is a brilliant investment."**
>
> **-B. Rhodes**

wedding day where you had a wedding fit for a modern-day princess. You want to be the talk of the town on your big day. Therefore, you are willing to work extra hours and make whatever financial investment required to make it happen. Yet the question remains, how much have you really invested into the marriage itself? How much work have you done on yourself in order to be ready for that ring? If you are willing to invest yourself, the return will be great, but only if you are *ready!*

What many ladies fail to realize is that there is a pre-requisite to getting married. You must already be a wife before you get that ring. There are sacrifices that you have to make, and you have to have a solid understanding of all that marriage entails. Unfortunately, a lot of people go into marriage ill-prepared and wind up make detrimental mistakes, particularly Christians. Getting married is taught to be the safer bet in order to avoid eternal punishment, and *that* is where the mistake is made. In an ill-advised effort to avoid eternal hell, you place yourself in and earthly hell. When all you really have to do is submit yourself unto Christ, and He will keep you! Keep your mind off the ring, and keep it on Christ; and you'll go a long way towards being ready!

Previously, we mentioned that you would have to ask yourself some tough questions. Aside from asking yourself if you truly want the ring, you have to go in depth to see if you're ready for marriage. Remember, to thine own self, be true!

Are you willing to understand and forgive, even when it's not **warranted?**

Let's face it, people are bound to make mistakes...men in particular. Sometimes, he will blindly make a mistake, and then there will be times when he does so blatantly. Perhaps there's an accident with finances, maybe he says something hurtful, or maybe he commits the unthinkable...infidelity. The question you must ask yourself here is, "Are you willing to understand and forgive, even in times like these, where you've done nothing wrong?" You see in marriage, sometimes you have to be willing to give up your right to *be* right. Yes, infidelity is in fact grounds for divorce. However, if you've resolved to stay in the marriage, you have to find out where things broke down so that you can understand the cause for the infidelity. Even if you decide *not* to stay, you still have to forgive, as being unforgiving will only hurt you in the long run and will keep you from entering into the presence of God. It's a tough pill to swallow, but you have to be willing to press past adversity and your own feelings, and put the feelings of your spouse first. Marriage requires sacrifice.

Are you willing to give, even if you receive nothing in return?

As a wife, you **must** be selfless. There may be times where you are giving to your spouse, and they are unable to give anything in return, and there will be times when the opposite is certainly true. This will be true in many different areas of your relationship; quality time, finances, or sex. Forgiveness is also one of those things that you may give, without receiving it in return. Keep in mind that this is the standard expectation once you accept that ring. You have to be willing to give selflessly, without expecting anything return. So, if you're in the courting stage of the relationship, heading up marriage, and you find that you're frequently giving without ever receiving anything in return, now would be a good time for you to think about taking a step back to reevaluate some things. Once you say "I do.", you have to stand on Galatians 6:9 which encourages, "And let us not be weary in well doing: for in due season we shall reap, if we faint not." You cannot get tired and stop giving, even if you don't receive anything in return.

> **"You have to be willing to press past adversity and your own feelings, and put the feelings of your spouse first. Marriage requires sacrifice."**

Are you ready to help, even if the trip turns into a journey?

We'll go back to the first question for a moment in order to gain a little insight. Let's say that infidelity occurs, and you've decided to forgive him and stay in the marriage. Now let's take this a step further and, say that after understanding the cause for the infidelity, you find out even more details regarding the incident. This may very well cause the road towards healing your marriage to take longer than a few months. Perhaps it takes a year, or several years!

Another example of the trip turning into a journey would be if there were a medical issue that leaves your spouse incapacitated in some way. You are now required to be the sole caregiver for your spouse and any children that you may have. This means there will be times when you have to go above and beyond to take care of your mate. So, what do you do if their journey to health takes longer than expected? Are you prepared to stay the course? We're sure that your answer was "yes". However, you also have to consider the fact that your mate will be unable to give back to you in the same capacity that you give to him. Therefore, you will be required give without receiving much, if anything at all, in return. Under any of these circumstances, are you willing to stay if that road to recovery takes a longer time than expected? In other words, will you be in it for the long haul?

Are you ready and willing to submit to a man?

You have to be both! It wouldn't surprise us if many women stopped reading here! However, this willingness and readiness to submit is a pre-requisite to marriage. Ephesians 5:22-23 says, "Wives, submit yourselves to your own husbands as you do to the Lord. For the husband is the head of the wife as Christ is the head of the church, his body, of which he is the Savior." Don't get the definition of submission misconstrued. Submission in this case is submission unto God, which applies to the husband, so don't feel that your submission as a wife is for his benefit! For husbands, submission to God means to honor Him and everything that he says. He tells men to treat their wives as the weaker vessel, and to love her as Christ loved the church. That sounds like a *benefit* for the wife! Christ died for the church, so husbands have to die for their wives daily in order to honor them.

Now let us be clear here, *subservience* and *submission* are two very different things. As the wife, it is up to you to help meet the needs of your husband. In no way does being submissive in

> **"Subservience and submission are two very different things."**

marriage mean that you must lay down and a door mat or that you are no longer entitled to have a voice or an opinion. Nor does submission mean that you cease from being fierce, wonderful, and powerful. True submission means that willfully make and intentional decision to take all of your greatness and all of your power and couple it with that of your husband. You must be intentional about placing your power up under the leadership of your husband and helping to propel him to his place of greatness. In doing so, he is able to lead your family to your collective place of destiny far quicker than he would ever be able to do alone. God commands that you submit to your husband. He has ordained submission to be a part of marriage.

Of course, anything that is ordained of God is great for the body. Because you are submissive to your husband in obedience to the command of God, if your husband doesn't treat you right, God has promised to not even hear the husband's prayers! That sounds like a benefit! This is what has been told to us through the word of God. Breaking the order of things brings damnation upon the house.

Are you ready to change your last name fully, and not make it a hyphenated name?

If you pressed your way through that submission piece and continued to read...Bravo! But, again we really would not be surprised if many of you stop reading at this point! Let's look at this whole hyphenated name thing through the lens of submission. Now you may be saying to yourself, "What in the world does keeping my last name have to do with submission? It's not like I'm not using my husband's last name at all!" And our answer to that is EVERYTHING! A hyphenated last name is not submission!

In most cases, at birth you were given your father's last name. In some cases, if your parents weren't married, then you were probably given your mother's last name. This is because your last name is symbolic to the person that you are submitted to. When you get married, you are no longer to be under submission to your parents. The Bible teaches that you should summit yourself to your husband. This means that taking on your husband's last name is symbolic of the fact that you are not submitted to him.

Now we have heard women say that they keep their last name for career reasons or to keep their father's name going. Our response to that is, either you trust God or you don't. We have to do things God's way, without compromise in order to truly be able to walk in our purpose. Keeping your last name going is not a part of your purpose. That is why you have brothers, uncles, and fathers! God did not ordain that the wife or the woman should be the one that carries on the lineage. That is not what you have been called to do, and you have to be okay with being in God's divine purpose.

James 1:5 says "If any of you lack wisdom, you should ask God, who gives generously to all without finding fault, and it will be given to you." If you really want the ring, ask God, and He will not turn you away! Proverbs 11:14 says "Where no counsel is, the people fall: but in the multitude of counselors, there is safety." Seek out the wisdom of those that are prosperous in their marriage and who have been down that road you are now on, and there will be safe places.

Marriage is your promise before God and family to love and to cherish your spouse for **better** and for **worse**. You promise to love them in **sickness**, and in **health**. That love persists whether you are **richer**, or **poorer**. It is also a covenant between two people until they are parted by **death**. After you say "I do", it becomes real. You can't say "I did"; "I do" is infinite, so it is everlasting. You have to find a way to make it work; you made a promise unto God. You reach the point of no return once you recite your vows!

So once again, do you really want the ring?

CHAPTER 2

Is It Really About the Ring?

"Do not be anxious about anything, but in every situation, by prayer and petition, with thanksgiving, present your requests to God."
Philippians 4:6

More often than not, women see themselves settle in relationships for many different reasons. When outsiders ask if marriage is in the picture, you have an excuse. You may say that you're not ready yet, but you know that you've had your dress and venue in mind since you were a little girl! Is the thought of the ring keeping you in that relationship? Is it really the ring that's keeping you there, when there are chances to move on and try again? If there's no bended knee in sight from the man in your life, what's keeping you there? We're willing to bet that you definitely have some things to consider now, and we'll go into those below. As always, when you ask yourself these questions, dig deep, look inwardly and be honest with yourself!

Do you realize that you deserve more?

You've been holding onto this relationship by a string. You've been allowing this man to lead you on, and there's no sign of him turning you into a wife. If he sees a jewelry store, he's already walking on the opposite side of the street! Unfortunately, we're sure many of you ladies can relate. You should know your worth, and demand your worth! The sad part to this question is that many of you may not realize that you deserve more. The alternative is that you have an idea that you deserve more, but you don't fully believe it. If you do realize that you deserve more than what you've received and you continue to stay, we have to ask....is it really about the ring? Some ladies stay because they feel that if they invest enough time, a change may occur, but again, is it really about the ring at that point? This leads right into the next question...

Are you afraid of starting over?

You've invested so much time, knowing that you've *wasted* that time. You're hoping against hope that your man will change and get over his phobia of commitment. Everything is screaming at you to move on, yet you have some time in this relationship. In fact, you may have a child with this man, and children from previous relationships. You ask yourself "Will anybody want me with children?" Chances are if you've been strung along for quite some time, that person has already shown you their intentions. Sadly, you realize that this is as good as it's going to get. At that point, you're thinking you might as well stay. Does it have something to do with being comfortable? Do you feel that you're too old to begin again? You're afraid to go through the courtship phase again with another man. In fact, you're afraid to get hurt even worse by someone new, so you stay. Worse yet, you may tell yourself that this man will marry you, and buy your own ring! Many of you ladies may think it sounds crazy, but it's happened! Don't stay with that man out of the fear of starting over!

Are you afraid of being alone?

A lot of women are so afraid of being abandoned that they stay in a relationship, hoping for a ring. Let us be clear on this one, being alone in a relationship is only one step above being alone altogether! If you suffer from abandonment issues, you may not be ready to admit it! This could stem from an early age. One parent or the other may not have been present, and so you are afraid of being abandoned, or even worse….you have no identity. Unfortunately, you then go out and find some comfort in *any* attention from the opposite sex, so long as it's something! You may think it's about the ring….but it's really that you don't want to be alone! It's infinitely better to love yourself, *by* yourself, than to stay in something that's leading nowhere!

Are you sabotaging progress because you're afraid?

There's a quote that comes to mind from Marianne Williamson.

> **"Our deepest fear is not that we are inadequate. Our deepest fear is that we are powerful beyond measure. It is our light, not our darkness that most frightens us."**
>
> **- Marianne Williamson**

There are many people that are afraid of failure. Believe it or not, there are also people that are afraid of success. You may say that you've never seen a successful marriage, so you'll make sure that you never get to that point! You're afraid because you won't know what to do! You have a man that wants to make you a wife, but even *this* is unfamiliar territory. You'll nip that idea in the bud before it has the chance to bloom. Ladies, let's be brutally honest for a moment. Sometimes, it's not the man's fault why there is no ring in sight.

You may have gone through *several* good men who actually wanted to marry you! Thus, it goes back to the original question; is it really about the ring? The last thing to ask in relation to the main question is…

Are you satisfied with being an afterthought?

You may be with a man that doesn't make you a priority in his life. He may not even want to put a title on what the two of you share! There isn't even a chance of going from "bae" to "bride". Sadly, it doesn't even get to the first point! If you don't invest in yourself, nobody will! The alternative is continuing to settle for "Netflix and chill", or late-night encounters. You don't have to accept what you're going through. Like we said before, some of you are doing well enough to court yourselves, and it happens! You may have been at your office and known a woman that's always getting nice flowers delivered. What you may not realize is that she's sending them to herself!

That may have been a bit of a blow, but the word of God heals all! For the healing, we'll take a look at Luke 12:6-7, which says, "Are not five sparrows sold for two copper coins? And not one of them is forgotten before God. But the very hairs of your head are all numbered. Do not fear therefore; you are of more value than many sparrows." What is there to fear when you are a child of God? He only has your best interests in mind. Don't settle for less than what God has to offer! This means working on you. You can't be so willing to offer others insight on their situations without first looking within.

> **"You are more valuable than any diamond."**

Is it really about the ring? Or are there some issues on the inside that need to be confronted? Those issues run deeper than the cost of a ring, and you are more valuable than the cost of any diamond.

CHAPTER 3

The Cost of the Ring

"For which of you, intending to build a tower, does not sit down first and count the cost, whether he has enough to finish it" Luke 14:28

Nothing in this life is free. In fact, everything has a cost. Just as you have to pay the cost to be the boss, you have to also pay the cost to be the bride. As Luke 14:28 says, "For which of you, intending to build a tower, does not sit down first and count the cost, whether he has *enough* to finish *it*—"When we apply that to relationships, dating and marriage, we know that the expected outcome to any courting is marriage. However, many ladies don't sit down and consider the cost. If you desire to get the ring, there will be a price. Ask yourself if you are you willing to pay that price to not only get the ring, but also keep it? Ladies, this is your season of singleness, and it's not a curse! It is a season of preparation and restoration! If you're truly single, it's a season of preparation. If you're divorced or widowed, then it's a season of restoration. That's something to keep in mind. If you want the ring, you have to have the due diligence to be prepared, so that you can pay the cost. With that said, here's the cost of that ring.

Ridicule is part of the cost.

Who would ridicule you, you may ask? You risk the ridicule of your friends, your spouse's friends. The ridicule of your family and your spouse's family will also be a part of that cost. There will be some dislike on both sides of the coin. As soon as things get uncomfortable and there are too many people talking, is that your cue to leave? In fact, you may get ridicule from the person you want to marry! If they've been hurt in the past, they may try to come at you, not to hurt your feelings, but to see if you have any staying power. If there's a gap in age, differences in ethnicity, religious backgrounds, or that person has baggage, people will have opinions, and they won't be quiet. Is that a cost you're ready to pay to become a wife?

> **"Your *Season of Singleness,* and it's not a curse! It is a season of preparation and restoration!"**
>
> **-Marriage of God**

Are you ready to pay the cost of opposition?

Let's get this one clear, opposition doesn't always come up in the form of other people. We're specifically talking about the spirits of fear and doubt. There is fear of the unknown. You could be experiencing doubt, wondering if you're ready, or if you're soon-to-be husband is ready. There may be some temptation as well in the form of another good-looking man that comes along. Are you prepared to deal with these forces? Trust us ladies, they will come, and they *must* come. Every relationship *must* be tested!

Are you ready to be scrutinized?

This is where a lot of you may want to cut out because you love your privacy! However, this has to happen! You have to know the man whom you've decided to bond covenants with eternally. Respectfully, that man has to know you as well! You don't want to put yourself in a situation where you don't have all the answers. So, as it's said today, you need receipts! The scrutiny only gets worse when you're dealing with your significant other's family! They'll want to know where you're from, your religious background, your occupations. This goes with the territory, so the scrutiny isn't always bad. Think of it as a double-edged sword. Let's be clear on this one though, there is such a thing as too much scrutiny, so keep that in mind! This is a life commitment, so you have to be ready and know your spouse inside and out.

Toleration is the cost.

Are you willing to tolerate the idiosyncrasies that make a person who they are? Can you tolerate small lies from him? Are you able to put up with his occasionally odd and childish behaviors? Is it within you to accept the fact that your man may have childhood friends that are female? You have to figure out what you'll tolerate, but you also have to figure out what you're *not* willing to tolerate. There should be some deal breakers, because boundaries must be set. Otherwise, you're inviting somebody to walk all over you, and that isn't good at all. If we may be brutally honest for a moment, the secret is that no man will ever be 100 percent of what you want. There will always be somebody that's better in some regard, but it's all about what you're willing to tolerate and accept. When considering what you will not tolerate, you have to figure out the cause of *why* you will not tolerate these things. You *must* know what you're willing to put up with from your husband, and what will make you walk away.

This will cost you your life.

We're not talking in the physical sense, in that you will have to give up your life for the ring. Wives take on their husband's last name when they get married. They will take on the priesthood of who God has destined their husbands to be. As Christ died for the church, husbands and wives must be willing to die to themselves daily. To give you more clarification, you have to be willing to die to your own selfish desires and ambitions, and your own will to be right all the time. You have to submit to him, daily. It means that you have to die to yourself, *daily*. When you get married, the two become one, so your life is no longer your own. There is an order of submission. Husbands must submit unto God, and wives must submit unto their husbands. Ladies, are you willing to give up who you are for the ring?

> **"You have to be willing to die to your own selfish desires and ambitions, and your own will to be right all the time."**

Look back to the word of God. Marriage is the tower you want to build. If you are in a relationship, do you have enough to finish that tower? You want the ring, but are you ready *and* willing to pay the cost? Do you have what it takes to be a wife to him? Are you ready to overcome the hurdles in order to buy that ring that you desire?

The ring has a cost, and it's an amount that can't be found in your bank account.

THE RING MASTER PLAN

CHAPTER 4

Is the Ring In Sight?

"You lust and do not have. You murder and covet and cannot obtain. You fight and war. Yet you do not have because you do not ask. You ask and do not receive, because you ask amiss, that you may spend *it* on your pleasures." (James 4:2-3)

When you hear the word "engage", or if you hear someone say that they are "engaged" in anything or with anyone, you automatically envision see the end. You have an expectation of where things will lead. If you are engaged in conversation, you have an expectation for where the conversation will lead. If you are engaged in a business venture, there is an expected outcome for that business venture.

43

You are engaged to a gentleman, you *expect* to get married to that man! You should always have an expectation. So, if you're giving of yourself, your time, your emotions, and a piece of your heart without an expectation for where this relationship will eventually lead, you may need to reassess the relationship.

Life is all about reciprocity. When you work a job, you expect to be paid. When you go to sleep, you expect to be rested. In parenting, you make certain sacrifices and you expect to raise model children. There's always an expected end. If there is no end in sight, or you are headed towards a dead end, it's okay to take a step back to reassess the route in order to determine if there is an expected end.

James 4:2-3 tells states, "You lust and do not have. You murder and covet and cannot obtain. You fight and war. Yet you do not have because you do not ask. You ask and do not receive, because you ask amiss, that you may spend it on your pleasures." Let's break down these verses and apply them to relationships so that you can gain some insight into the marriage relationship.

You lust and you do not have. The lust is for the ring, yet you don't have it. **You murder and covet and cannot obtain. You fight and war.** Murder in this case is the murdering of your spirit, so that you can fulfill the lustful desires of your flesh. You've given him your mind, body and heart, yet you still have not obtained the ring. You may fight and war with your man and with the spirit of God within you. **You ask and do not receive, because you ask amiss, so that you may spend it on your pleasures.** You are not intentional in the questions that you ask him. They serve no purpose other than to satisfy your own fleshly gain. You shy away from asking any questions necessarily in pursuit of bringing glory to God through the covenant of marriage.

Instead of being deliberate in your pursuit of marriage, you dance around the subject with the man in your life. You casually mention that one of your friends just got engaged, and that her ring is sooo beautiful. You mention that you've been invited to a classmate, co-worker, or sorority sister's wedding. These conversations must have a point! You will get nowhere fast unless you're willing to travel on a definite path. If you have an expected outcome in all of your other endeavors, then surely there should be an expected outcome to your relationship. These expectations need to be shared with the man that desires to spend time with you.

You know in your spirit that you are worth a far greater level of commitment than you've been settling for. If you feel as though the ring should be in sight, yet it's nowhere to be found, you may want to ask your beau the questions listed below. Try being as nonconfrontational as possible. You don't even need to stir up negative emotions with these questions. Don't allow anger to intensify the conversation if he refuses to give you straight answer. Remember Proverbs 15:1, which says, "A soft answer turneth away wrath: but grievous words stir up anger." There's no need to stir up anger within him or yourself. All you need to do is be intentional about asking the right questions and honestly judge his answers.

"How do you see me?"

There's nothing wrong with gaining clarification on the direction of your relationship. Though there may be a few bumps along the road, you should be able to see the end of the road...your expected end. There will undoubtedly be storms, but you should know the expected result. If you're dealing with a man who won't even put a label on what the two of you have together, that's a definite red flag! He may attempt to avoid the question or try to buy time by asking, "What do you mean?" Do not get discouraged or distracted. Remember your goal is simply to determine where the ring is. Both of you should have clearly defined expectations, and you must share them to make sure that both of you are on the same page.

> **"There's nothing wrong with gaining clarification on the direction of your relationship."**

To be honest, in as little as a couple of months a man knows whether he wants to take the relationship down the road leading to marriage. He has considered this question in his heart long before you ever work up the nerves to ask the question. If he has a clear understanding of where you stand in his life, he'll give you the answer that leans towards the ring. Even if his answer does not lean towards marriage, it's great for you to find out sooner rather than later. At any rate, it's always good to make sure that you two are traveling down the same road, and in the same direction.

"How do you see us?"

This is a natural progression from the first question. As we mentioned before, you have an expected result for any endeavor. After establishing how your man

> **"In as little as a couple of months a man knows whether he wants to take the relationship down the road leading to marriage."**

feels about you, you should see where his feelings are concerning the two of you together. If he says something like, "We're living in the moment", or asks, "Why are you pressing me?", beware. Keep those eyes and ears open ladies! Just to be clear, this is not an automatic red flag. People get on the defensive when they feel as though they are being cornered. Just keep your eyes open. Stay alert. Remember, clarity goes a long way, and the way he answers can tell you a lot.

"Where do you see us going from here?"

Having established where you stand in his life, and where he stands on the direction of the relationship, this is quite naturally your next question. Life is a journey. Your body, heart and spirit are the parts that make up the vehicle, and the man is the driver. You want to make sure the driver has mapped out a clear route to the destination. As we stated before, there's **absolutely** *nothing* wrong with clarification! It bears repeating, but if you don't get the answer you expect, don't go running for the hills just yet. Keep your eyes open for any other signs that the ring may *not* be in sight. Regardless of whether or not you feel that things may be going in the right direction, here's the next question that you should ask…

"Do you have any projections?"

Not everyone has a clear plan for their life. Some people may not always know exactly what they want. However, for those who do know what they want, they also have a preferred timeframe and plan for achieving the things they desire sooner rather than later. Asking this question helps you to gain clarity on the pace at which your man is moving towards the ring, if he is even moving towards it at all. This question may put him on the defensive once again, so don't get overly upset if you don't get a definitive answer. However, you can tell a lot about where his expectations lie just by understanding his established timeline for getting to the expected end. The final question you may want to ask is…

"What are your expectations of me?"

Life based off of expectations. If you drink a tall glass of water, you expect for your thirst to be quenched. If you watch a person's live stream, you expect entertainment or useful content. If you are in a relationship with a man, you should expect the relationship to progress towards marriage. Sadly, this doesn't always happen. Even the most basic of expectations are never established up front! These expectations should be the foundation on which the relationship is built. If he can't provide you with the basics and lay a foundation, then you should not be looking to build a future with this man!

If you're starting to feel as though the ring may not be in sight, it's important that you ask those questions. Again, these are not meant to be confrontational, but you deserve honest insight and clarity as to whether or not your significant other is willing to travel down the same road that you're traveling on. Overall, these questions allow you to determine if are in a meaningful relationship or if you are wasting your time. Again, if you don't get the desired responses, don't be discouraged. It's okay. Naturally, people get defensive when you start asking questions that make them uncomfortable. Be mindful that your approach to presenting these questions will mean the difference between getting the answers you need, and getting the run around.

You may be asking, "When is the right time to ask these questions?" The truth is that there is no set time, but the sooner the better. Nobody likes to have their time wasted. Some of you may feel comfortable enough to ask these questions within the first few weeks of the courtship. While it may take others longer. Trust your heart, and trust God. He will never steer you wrong! These questions are your indicator to whether or not marriage is on his radar or if the ring is in sight. You need to know whether to run to the bridal store, or run for the hills...and no one will blame you for that!

> **"You need to know whether to run to the bridal store, or run for the hills."**

CHAPTER 5

The Importance of the Ring

"There are three things that amaze me—no, four things that I don't understand: how an eagle glides through the sky, how a snake slithers on a rock, how a ship navigates the ocean, how a man loves a woman."

How many times have you seen a nice wedding ring on a woman's finger, and you find yourself at a loss for words because it looks just that amazing? It's alright to be honest about it. This still happens to both of us! However, where many singles make their mistake is they get so enamored with the thought and glamour of the ring, that they forget about everything else that goes along with being the recipient of the ring. We're sure most of you have found out that the whole ideology that bigger the ring is, the better the marriage is false. The truth of the matter is, if you get a extravagant ring, you'll show it off, but the meaning behind the ring runs deeper than its size. From a man's perspective, you have to consider the time and effort that he's putting into selecting and being able to purchase that ring. It symbolizes that a man really cares, and wants to go to the next level. Beyond picking the ring out, it takes a man time to get to the point of offering a ring (and hopefully it is for the right reasons)!

Instead of focusing on the size of the ring, focus on its importance, and the symbolism behind the ring. There are so many things that the act of a man presenting his woman with a ring symbolizes. These are the things

> **"Don't get so enamored with the thought and glamour of the ring, that you forget about everything else that goes along with being the**

that you should draw your focus to because at the end of the day. It is these things that will matter most to the relationship...regardless to how big or how small the actual ring may be.

A ring symbolizes the maturation of the relationship.

When someone gets engaged, without them ever saying a word, everyone around them instantly knows what a ring means. It symbolizes that you and your significant other are taking this relationship seriously. A ring is a silent statement that puts an end to shacking up, Netflix and chill, or whatever the case may be. The ring speaks louder than a title ever could. In the previous chapter, we brought up some questions that you might ask to determine if the ring is in sight; nothing can answer those questions like actually receiving the ring! The ring is a statement piece that says, "this man is serious about you, and doesn't mind letting the world know that you two are together". Ladies, that expected end that you've envisioned is closer than you think when a ring is presented.

The ring symbolizes that he is no longer playing small.

Traditionally, men propose to women, so the ring symbolizes that he's no longer playing small. When a man plays small, the sacrifices he is willing to make are small, but when he plays big he willingly makes a bigger sacrifice for you. Respect is extremely important to men, and it is one thing that a man does not take lightly. His money is just as important to him.

While dinner dates and movies are nice and can be romantic, they are small financial sacrifices that do not require any real commitment. An investment in a ring, on the other hand, requires more than an overtime check. To do something of this magnitude takes a plan and requires that he make a big sacrifice. The purchase of a ring means that he is committing to more than a small two-hour commitment or a small investment. Anything that requires a financial commitment of more than three paychecks, is no longer an impromptu play. It requires a definite game plan.

When it comes to playing small, asking a question like "What are you doing Friday night?" is not a big deal. However, when a man asks, "What are you doing for the rest of your life? And would you like to spend it with me?" These questions are a

big deal. This man is no longer satisfied with playing small. He's making a big play. To risk being vulnerable to someone else's response - without you knowing how they will answer- this is a major play for a man. The ring and the process shows that he is committed to playing big.

Rings symbolize the entering into of a covenant.

On that glorious day, when you get to the altar, the you both will recite your wedding vows, and both the man and the woman will get a ring. Therefore, it's an equal exchange of the vows. You are bound to those vows, and to that person, as your two lives become one. When women see a good-looking man, her gaze will most likely go to his hands to see if there is a ring present. Why? Because she's cannot simply look into his eyes to see if he has exchanged vows with anyone yet. The ring is a visual symbol that he has entered into covenant with someone already. The outcome of her inspection determines her future interactions with that man. Now, this isn't to say that if there's no ring in sight, then that gentleman isn't married. There are many men who not trying to be dishonest and have legitimate reasons for not wearing their rings. Even if the ring is lost or damaged, the covenant that you exchanged with your spouse doesn't diminish.

> **"The wedding ring is a visual symbol that one has entered into covenant with someone else."**

The ring symbolizes that you are loved!

This is where last verse in our reference scripture stands out. These were the words of King Solomon, who was held in high regard for his wisdom. In fact, King Solomon is known as the wisest man to ever live. Yet, even he was unable to understand the phenomena of love that a man has for the women who wins his heart.

When a woman has truly won the heart of a man, the love that he feels towards her goes beyond mere words. It's something that is not easily explained...it has to be experienced. This is the thing that would cause a man to willingly lay down his life to the love of his life. It's this intense emotion that would cause a man to do any and everything in his power to honor and protect the one who has captured his heart.

Even in today's society, we may come up short when trying to understand that love, but we can certainly feel it! The truth of the matter is that we all desire to be loved in such a way. Women have been taught about and longing for that kind of love from a very young age. Very early on we learn that the ring is an outward expression of someone else's love towards you! It symbolizes that this man thinks that you are important enough and special enough to become one with you. Let's face it, it's a big deal when you get a man to give you a ring.

In the grand scheme of things, the size of the ring is irrelevant. It's all about the symbolism behind it. You can have the love, exchange of covenant, and a maturation of the relationship without the ring; you can have a rubber band or some string on your finger! It all boils down to the symbolization behind it.

All that the ring stands for hold meaning.

If you still think that the ring doesn't have importance, consider this:

Why is that before an act infidelity is committed, most people take their ring off?

Why does this happen? Is it an act of guilt? Is it a result of the shame of willfully dishonoring the marital covenant? We are not sure if there are many people alive that can properly explain that action. On the other hand, people are quick to tell you that if he wanted to keep you, he should've put a ring on your finger. What would be the point, if no one understood the importance of the ring?

> **"The flashiest ring in the world doesn't matter if you don't understand what it means to be offered the ring in the first place."**

The flashiest ring in the world doesn't matter if you don't understand what it means to be offered the ring in the first place.

CHAPTER 6

The Ring and the Thing

"He who is slow to anger is better than the mighty. And he who rules his spirit, than he who takes the city." (Proverbs 16:32)

At some point, everyone desires physical intimacy. This presents a problem for women in particular, who were taught from an early age to abstain until you have the ring. You've heard it in some way, shape, or form! "Keep the legs closed!" "Don't give up the cookies!" The problem is that your body, heart and hormones will betray you. In fact, you will want to do everything *except* for abstaining. After a while, some ladies eventually give in and have sex. The next thing you know, you're left feeling guilty and praying that God will restore you and forgive you for going against what you were taught by your parents and from the word of God.

As a married couple, we understand your dilemma!

> **"The problem remaining abstinent is that your body, heart and hormones will betray your mind."**

You see, our oldest son was born out of wedlock. We had him while we were both still in college and "shacking up". During this time in our lives, we were living totally outside of the will of God and we did so for quite some time. It took us going through some very rough times before we decided to do things God's way. There was a point in time where Brent was incarcerated and spent for four years in prison. During this 4-year period, I got saved and this time I earnestly surrendered my life to the Lord. After Brent came home, I was bound and determined to continue to live my life in a way that honored God. We courted in abstinence for over a year before we got married. It became extremely difficult to abstain from our sexual desires during that time of courtship, but it was not impossible! There will be triggers that set you off and you will definitely be tested. However, it is possible to exercise self-control.

One of the ways to exercise self-control is knowing your triggers, and knowing who can pull those triggers. All isn't lost if you've already

> **"Receiving the ring tend to make abstaining from our sexual desires even more difficult."**

made that mistake and given in to the temptation. It's okay and it happens! Remember, we were in your position at one point! The best thing you can do is realize you've made a mistake, repent to God, and ask Him to restore you. Allow Him to keep you in grace, so that you may do things the right way and be in His glory!

We whole-heartedly understand that celibacy before marriage isn't an easy thing, but consider if you will the downsides to giving in to temptation. Suppose you're dealing with a man who knows your triggers well and being a red-blooded man, he put on what we like to call "the full-court press". Let's be honest here. No matter how saved a man is, if given the opportunity, he WILL try you. Once you've given in, all respect for you and your standards goes out of the window. He now knows he can pull those triggers and get what he wants; the chase is over! Laying aside your standards puts you in the category of all of the other "on the fence" Christians. You have to fight the good fight! The "cookie" we referred to earlier; ladies, THAT is your bargaining chip! Once it's given away, you no longer have the advantage!

Again, we understand! We've been there! We've been together for 28 years, and were living together without the ring for 10 of those years. Our oldest son was born outside of wedlock; something had to give! We ultimately decided to do it God's way, and we are stronger because of it! It can be the same for you!

To get right down to it, there is a tie that is strengthened when you have sex. It begins to form when you start to engage in a conversation, yet you are unaware of it. You are tied to that individual; it is not just sex. This is why it is important to learn how read between the lines, and decipher what men say from what they mean. Recognizing that tie will help you to abstain from those desires and realize your worth! Men and women think differently; so it's not always about men trying to take advantage of you and then leave. However, it's difficult to determine who's genuine, and who has an ulterior motive!

Trust us; we understand the difficulties of celibacy. It challenges you to the core. However, it also forces you to discipline yourself and to structure your life in order for you to be found and be ready to become a wife. Giving into you desires allows a man to keep you living in that "gray area". You'll be expected to act behave like a wife, without the ring! He will keep you as "bae" while he keeping you at bay! Proverbs 16:32 can definitely help you put things into perspective;

"He who is slow to anger is better than the mighty. And he who rules his spirit, than he who takes the city."

You must learn how to rule your spirit. If you don't, no one will respect it…not even you?

THE RING MASTER PLAN

CHAPTER 7

When Not to Accept the Ring

Wisdom is the principle thing; therefore, get wisdom: and with all thy getting get understanding. Proverbs 4:7

So far, we've been doing a lot of talking about getting the ring. We've spoken about the cost of the ring, determining if the ring is something you really want, the importance of the ring, among other things. We've talked about the beauty of marriage, and what is expected of you as a wife. You should prepare yourself to be a wife so that you can be found by a man of God when the time is right. However, with all of this talk about the ring we would be remiss if we didn't

67

BRENT & ANGEL RHODES

address the fact that not all proposals are sincere and not all relationships are God's best for you. While we absolutely support you in your quest to get the ring, there are times in life and relationship where you have to just say "No". What we are saying is that there may be an instance where you should *not* accept the ring.

> ## "Not all proposals are sincere and not all relationships are God's best for you."

Let us be clear here, we are not telling you to say no if you are *truly* ready to become a wife or if you are just nervous about the unknown. What happens a lot with single ladies is that out of wanting to serve their own vain desires, they end up staying in relationships far longer than they should. They stay in the relationship with "Mr. Wrong", or "Mr. Right Now", but not "Mr. Right For Me" that was sent to you from God. In fact, many of these ladies know it deep within their heart of hearts that they shouldn't stay! Not everything that glitters is gold, and a good idea isn't necessarily equate to a *God* idea. It's okay to focus on getting the ring, but you shouldn't endeavor to get the ring by any means necessary. As you continue, headed in the right direction, along the road to marriage, be sure that you use your peripheral vision to spot those warning signs that indicate danger ahead.

Your *Season of Singleness*, should be a glorious time in your life, but you may be focused on out other things. Perhaps your focused on the fact that your biological clock is

> **"You may think that he's Mr. Right For Me, but he may simply be Mr. Right Now!"**

ticking. Or maybe your pouring all of your energy into solving the great mystery of "When will I find a man?" When you meet someone, you may think that he's Mr. Right For Me, but as we said before, he may simply be Mr. Right Now! Sometimes we can desire things that make us feel good, are not good for our spirit. The things that feel good *to* us are not always good *for* us. Do not chase after the updated relationship status and the ring at the expense of your spiritual wellbeing. You should always listen to the voice of God instead of going with the status quo. So, the question remains, when should you *not* accept the ring?

If he will not commit to a time frame, don't accept the ring!

By no means are we saying that he has to have an exact date in mind. Don't expect him to present you with the ring and say "Let's get married on November 18th, 2018". However, you should expect a time frame as to when he plans to make you his wife. Believe it or not, some men actual the act of giving you a ring as a tactic to keep you quiet! Afterwards, he might say that you have the ring, so you two can work out the time frame out later. Don't be afraid to test the waters on this one. You can put out a time frame, let's say 12 months. If he counters with a time frame that is reasonable to what you suggested, say 18 months, you guys are on the right track. Having him commit to a time frame ensures that he is held accountable to his actions. Otherwise, he's just playing with you and leading you on. That's a red flag! If he doesn't have any time frame in mind, don't accept the ring!

Do not accept a ring from him if he is still discussing "her"!

> # If he doesn't have any time frame in mind, don't accept the ring!

A lot of you ladies may be asking, "Who is 'her'?" "Her" is the ex-girlfriend. If she is still coming up in your conversations chances are she is at the forefront of his mind, and he is not over her! If in fact, he's still discussing her and they went through a bad breakup, you are setting yourself up to pay for "her" mistakes. You see, until he's over her, he will continue to rehearse the problems that he experienced with "her" and anything that you do will remind him of all of the bad times her experienced with "her". Whatever a man meditates on in his heart is what his reality will be (Proverbs 23:7). If you start to reconsider taking your relationship with him to the next level due to his conversation constantly revolving around "her", he may offer you a ring out of his fear of losing you. Don't accept it!

71

If he is not respecting your current courtship, do not accept the ring!

It is imperative that you set some very clear boundaries within the courtship. This means that you have to set your standards and make them known up front. If this man tries to pressure you into lowering your standards, it's a definite red flag! If he disrespects or disregards the boundaries of the courtship, you can only expect more of the same within your marriage. As we stated in the last chapter, sex is a very important part of the marriage. However, it is something that you should only enjoy within the covenant of marriage. You should not engage in sex during the courtship. If he continuously tries to push your buttons to get you to give in, there may be danger ahead! If he uses the ring as an excuse to no longer regard your sexual boundaries, there is definitely danger ahead. If he doesn't respect you now, chances are that he won't respect you after you accept that ring. By accepting the ring when he's disrespecting your standards and disregarding your boundaries, you are telling him "I'm okay with the way you treat me now."

There may be times when the ring is presented, and your mind and heart will be screaming "Yes", but your spirit will be screaming "No! No! No!" During those times, you *must* listen to the spirit! It will lead you to all truth and will not steer you wrong! That which is ordained of God will be good for your mind, heart *and* spirit! You may have a selfish desire to accept the ring, but you have to know the warning signs of when *not* to accept it.

CHAPTER 8

While You Are Waiting on The Ring...

"For still the vision awaits its appointed time;
it hastens to the end – it will not lie.
If it seems slow, wait for it;
it will surely come; it will not delay."
Habakkuk 2:3

O f course, we realize that "waiting" is not a very popular word or concept...especially when spoken to single women who desire to be married. However, every woman who are working on herself and endeavoring to position herself for marriage needs to know the information in this chapter. So, it is our prayer that you have decided to fight the urge to skip this particular chapter and read it in its entirety.

While you may not really enjoy this waiting period, it is an inevitable part of this *Season of Singleness.* And the things that you do...or fail to do in this season can directly affect the how long this season lasts. We cannot stress this enough, your *Season of Singleness* is your time of preparation or restoration.

So, while you are waiting for the ring, you need to consider a few things. The first thing you need to figure out is your single vision. For many of you the whole concept of a single vision is a foreign one, but it is one that you need to get acquainted with.

What is your vision for your season of singleness? What are the things that you dream of accomplishing that do not include a husband or family? Where do you desire to travel?

> **"The whole concept of a single vision is a foreign one, but it is one that you need to get acquainted with."**

Maybe you want to complete your degree or perhaps you are working on restoring your credit. This is the ideal time to take that "girlfriend getaway" that you and your bbf's have been putting off. When do you plan to finish your book? Most importantly, what is the status of your relationship with God? This is the time for you to develop and perfect your relationship with God, so that He can show you his purpose and plans for your life, future, and marriage.

What is your vision for your relationship? What are the things that you envision when you think of your marriage or your family? You need to look beyond the family movie nights. Where do you see yourself and your mate financially, where will you live and where will you worship?

Even though the vision that God has given you has not yet come to fruition, wait for it! By no means does **delayed** mean **denied**! As the old adage goes, "Good things come to those who wait." While you can believe that for other people, ladies often struggle with believing that it's true for themselves. What you must realize is that if good things can happen for other people that wait, they can happen for you!

> ## "What happens far too often is that we allow our sight to get in the way of our faith."

You should walk by faith, not by sight. What happens far too often is that we allow our sight to get in the way of our faith. We get so engulfed in what we see in front of us that we no longer focus on and believe for what God has already shown us will come to pass. We lose hope in that vision because we only use our eyes, and that my dear is *not* faith! As Hebrews 11:1 says, "Faith is the substance of things hoped for, it is the evidence of things not seen." Yet the Bible *also* says that faith without works is dead. Therefore, you *must* do the work! While you're in your *Season of Singleness*, there is work that must be done in order to bring your vision into fruition. As we said before, your *Season of Singleness* is that of preparation *and* restoration. You have to *prepare* yourself to be made a wife! The key is to strengthen your faith so that you don't lose sight of that vision!

While you're waiting for the ring, you have to get a few things in order.

You must realize that the ring does not define you!

You are not defined by your ring or the lack thereof. You are not defined by its size or price. More than anything, please

> "The key is to strengthen your faith so that you don't lose sight of that vision!"

know that you are not defined by your relationship status! What defines you is the person that you're building yourself to become, and who God has preordained you to be. You can't allow yourself to fall into the mental trap of believing that without a ring, your life has no value and you have made no real accomplishments. Because you haven't received the ring yet, does not mean that there's something wrong with you! This is also true for men as well. Men tend to define themselves by their occupation. When you ask a man who he is, he will tell you his occupation. As a woman, you are fearfully and wonderfully made in God's image. Don't get depressed as you wait for your expected end! Your status does not detract from who you are!

Find out who you are, and be made whole!

Until you know who *you* are, you can't expect anyone else to recognize you as his good thing. A lot of people walk around broken and have no clue about how to be made whole. They don't know who they are. You must figure out who you are, and why you are in this stage in your life. That is one of the most critical steps that should be accomplished while waiting for the ring! Marriage isn't a half of a man and a half of a woman coming together to make one whole person; it is two **WHOLE** people coming together as one! You have to make sure you do the due diligence to figure out who you are, and who God intended for you to be. By doing this, you allow Him to make you whole, so that you can be ready to be made a wife. This process is not easy. It will challenge you and force you out of your comfort zone. It is the medicine that you don't want to ingest, but it will make you all the better.

This process requires you to be naked, but not in the physical sense. You have to be completely open and honest with both God and with yourself. You can't change your past, but you can change yourself. At the end of the day, the only person that you can *truly* change is yourself! There may be so many things that have been burrowed deep inside of you that have caused you put up walls. In order to be made whole, you have to overcome these issues and break down the walls. While you wait for that marriage and that ring, while you are waiting for your "Boaz", work on being whole within yourself! Work on being Ruth!

Know that you are worth the wait!

You are far too valuable to base the rest of your life by rushing to a quick decision! The words of Proverbs 18:22 defines your worth clearly! They read, "He who finds a wife finds a good thing, and obtains favor from the Lord." Know that **you are favor**! You should never feel as though a man is doing you a favor by being in a relationship with you. As a wife, you are a prize, and a wonderful prize at that!

Remember Beautiful, this is a season of preparation and restoration. Some women may not want marriage, and that is okay! However, for those that do desire to be married, you want to be prepare for when that special person does comes along wanting to give you the ring! Until that time, some housekeeping is in order. You can have faith that you will find the one to give you that ring. However, without committing to doing the work...nothing will come to fruition.

CHAPTER 9

The Beauty of the Ring

"Finally brethren, whatsoever things are true, whatsoever things are honest, whatsoever things are just, whatsoever things are pure, whatsoever things are lovely, whatsoever things are of good report; if there be any virtue, and if there be any praise, think on these things." Philippian 4:8

When we think of the ring, and all that it entails, beauty is the one word that comes to mind. Beauty is an autological word, meaning it describes itself. In most situations where you think of the ring, you immediately think of its size. When walking into a jewelry store, your eyes will first lock onto the ring that has the biggest stone. When you think of your wedding ring, you take the number of carats into

> **"When you truly think about the beauty of the ring, and what it represents, your perception about the ring will change."**

consideration and most likely you come up with something grand; and there's nothing wrong with that! However, when you truly think about the beauty of the ring, and what it represents, your perception about the ring will change. You should try letting go of the preconceived notions that you've developed regarding the beauty of the ring, and look at what the true beauty behind the ring is.

> **"Oftentimes, when we say "beauty", we tend to make it synonymous with perfection. This can be problematic in love and relationships."**

We should take that correct perception into account. Oftentimes, when we say "beauty", we tend to make it synonymous with perfection. This can be problematic in love and relationships. Since everyone have varied perceptions, your idea of perfection will differ. The beauty of the ring transcends merely the materials used to make the ring or number of carats in the stone. There is absolutely nothing wrong with wanting a nice ring, but the beauty of the ring runs much deeper than that. The size of the ring does not equate to the beauty of the ring. However, that perception of the beauty of the ring only uses your sight to see the ring! It has no bearing on the true beauty!

The aesthetics of the ring have no bearing on its beauty!

> **"You want everything to be perfect in that special moment. What you should really focus on is being in the**

Ladies tend to get all wrapped up into the look of the ring. The same thing holds true for the wedding. You want everything to be perfect in that special moment. What you should really focus on is being in *the moment*! Think of it this way. There are two women whom were made wives. One woman has a half-carat ring that shows signs of rust, and the other woman has a 7-carat ring that's sparkling and new. The woman with the half-carat ring is going on strong for 20 years with her husband, whereas the woman with the 7-carat ring may have gotten divorced in a year's time! Don't get blinded with your physical sight! Marriage says, "'til death do us part", so the physical appearance of the ring should not matter. More often than not, those will the smaller rings understand the true implications behind marriage.

There is a rich culture within the ring!

When you consider what marriage is, you are joining your *entire* life with a man. That's why it's extremely important that you ensure that your new life is about to start with someone who hold the same beliefs that you do! He will make you legal in the eyes of God, because above all else he wants to honor God by honoring you. He wants to bring you into God's glory. Every household has its own set of rules and its own culture. The beauty of the ring is that the two of you are bringing your individual backgrounds, cultures, and traditions together under one roof where you get create a new culture and new traditions for your family.

There is a social beauty within the ring!

Marriage is the bedrock of a community, and the community is the foundation of society. The beauty of the ring is that it will cause you to take the vows of your covenants seriously. Your community is watching you, so you'll want to make sure that you set a good example for them to follow. In fact, people will watch you whether you want them to or not! Other people are looking at your marriage for hope that things will work out in their own marriages. A happy and healthy marriage leads to strong churches. Strong churches lead to strong communities and societies!

As you think about the beauty of the ring, keep Philippians 4:8 in mind.

"Finally brethren, whatsoever things are true, whatsoever things are honest, whatsoever things are just, whatsoever things are pure, whatsoever things are lovely, whatsoever things are of good report; if there be any virtue, and if there be any praise, think on these things."

The size and sparkle of the ring is nice, but the true beauty runs deeper than the number of carats.

The beauty of the ring is that the two of you are bringing your individual backgrounds, cultures, and traditions together under one roof where you get create a new culture and new traditions for your family.

CHAPTER 10

What's the Ring Costing You

"For which of you, desiring to build a tower, does not sit down first and count the cost, whether he has **enough** *to complete – otherwise, he has laid a foundation, and is not able to finish, all who see it will begin to mock him." Luke14:28-29*

"What is the ring costing me?! Absolutely NOTHING!" "Paying for my own ring? I'd never do that!" That's right...we heard you. Some of you ladies are probably wondering what we're talking about.

Believe it or not, many women have and some of you still are! That may say that is not be your claim to fame, but we have some news for you. Many of you *are* paying for your ring!

Stay with us, and let us explain. While you may not be paying monetarily for your ring, you're still paying nonetheless. In fact, you are paying a higher cost than the ring is actually worth. You are paying with something you don't have enough money to pay for! The price you pay is also something that you cannot get back!

You can spend money and make more money, but

> **"You give away pieces of yourself that cannot be given back."**

you can never recoup the value that you are spending for the ring. You see, you give away pieces of yourself that cannot be given back. We touched on the cost of the ring a bit in a previous chapter. Now let's talk about the hidden fees that you end up paying in your quest to be given the ring.

Luke14:28-29 reminds us that all things have a price. When you enter into a relationship with a man, you go out with him. Once people have seen you with him for a length of time, they begin to see you as a pair. After awhile, people will begin to wonder why your relationship hasn't moved towards that expected end. This causes your mind to start racing, and you begin to wonder what you need to do in order to get the ring. You begin to ponder "What more do I need to give of myself to prove my love to him?"

The mere fact that you think that you have to prove your love in order to get to that expected end, you're selling yourself short! Giving him your love should be enough. You should not compromise and give up who you are. Some single ladies will sometimes stop at nothing to get that ring so that they can put a stop to the ridicule! On the other hand, men are bargain hunters. They will attempt to get what they want and sacrifice the least of themselves to do so. It takes a mature man to willingly pay the full price. Ladies, what else is the ring costing you?

You pay with your time!

You meet a young man, he's nice-looking, and seems to have a lot going for himself. He approaches you, and you give him your conversation, to start. Before you part ways, you give him your number. Because you see potential in this man, you give him your time. If he calls you, you answer immediately. If you call, you may have to wait for him to answer or wait around for him to return your call. He might call you back, or he might not. The bottom line is that you give him *all* of your time in the hope that he will one day prove himself worthy and faithful. Yet the fact remains, you've given that man your time, and you will never be able to get it back! The more you avail yourself to a man before he proves himself worthy, the lower the price the man is willing to pay to win you over! If you find yourself in a situation where you give all of your time, and you get very little time in return, maybe you need to take a step back and really think about that relationship.

If you want a comparison, think about sales. Let's say that you go to a yard sale and you spot a rare and valuable painting. You ask the price and the owner tells you they realize the value, but they are only want $5 for the painting. Would you give them any more than the asking price just because you know that the painting is worth more? Chances are you would pay the $5 and take the painting before the owner came to their senses. This is the same way a man will respond to you if you go in giving too much of yourself too soon. It's not that he doesn't know that you are valuable. However, most men are not going to value you more than you value yourself.

"Men are bargain hunters!"

You pay by giving your heart prematurely.

We told you in the previous point that, you've readily availed yourself to a man, without equal exchange. After you've given your time, the next comes your heart. You start to do with this man that you shouldn't do and you begin to share things with him that you should because he hasn't proven to you that he is worthy of these things. Single ladies tend to run fast towards that ring, because a part of them doubts that it will ever come to them. Unfortunately, they end up going too far too fast and they give too much of themselves too soon. Before the you know it, the man knows everything about you, and you know very little about him. You've given him all the ammo and he knows exactly which of your buttons to press! So, you may not have paid a monetary cost for the ring, but you've lost a part of your heart. Your heart is far more valuable!

You pay by giving away yourself!

You give yourself to a man, and the truth of the matter is that he may not have any intentions on marrying you. To be quite honest,

> **"Most men are not going to value you more than you value yourself."**

why should he marry you? You're already doing the works of a wife without the ring, so he has no reason to marry you. You've given him your precious time. You've given him your heart by confiding in him. You've given him your most precious position by having sex with him. You've given him your spirit by giving him all of those things without doing it God's way. There are bits and pieces of you that walk away with each man at the end of the relationship. Just remember, that every man wants to have sex, yet they all also want to marry a virgin! Your body is a down payment with no refunds!

> **Any man sent to you from God will never lead you outside of the will of God!**

Any man sent to you from God will *never* lead you outside of the will of God! A true man of God is submitted to Him, and he's already walking in the authority of a husband, to lead you from courtship into marriage. He is already a husband when he finds you, and he will cover you spiritually even in courtship! In your *Season of Singleness* make sure that you are not paying the cost of the ring by being with someone who is unwilling to pay full price and do it God's way!

CHAPTER 11

Things to Discuss Before Considering the Ring

"Again I say to you that if two of you agree on earth concerning anything that they ask, it will be done for them by My Father in heaven." Matthew 18:19

Your *Season of Singleness* is all about preparation and restoration. It is preparation if you are single and you need to make yourself into a wife, so that you are ready when your husband finds you. It is about restoration if you are divorced, or unfortunately a widow. Many single ladies may think this season is a curse, but it is actually just the opposite. This season of your life is a blessing. It should be one of the most exciting times in your life, because it allows you to have uninterrupted time with God and freedom for yourself to grow! It's your time to spend with God, and build a strong foundation with Him so that He may replenish and restore you, transforming you into a wife. Even if you don't want to get married, you should still prepare! If you just shift your perspective, God will shift and begin to move things on your behalf. Before you consider courting, engagement, and marriage, you should be willing to have some honest discussions about these stages of relationships so that you're not completely at a loss when it is time for the ring!

Communication is key and it is very imperative to the health of any relationship. It's all about the agreement. We have to be in agreement on certain things before we even consider traveling down the road towards engagement, and ultimately to marriage.

> **"Communication is key and it is very imperative to the health of any relationship."**

The first thing to be considered is theology.

The Bible does say that we should not be unequally yoked with non-believers. It is best to make sure that you're both of the same spiritual and theological beliefs. Marriage is difficult and it is a lot more difficult when your religious beliefs are different! It's not impossible, but it does make things extremely difficult, and it is unbiblical. Your belief systems may not be compatible, so you definitely need to make sure you are on one accord spiritually.

> **Marriage is difficult, and it is a lot more difficult when you have differing religious beliefs."**

Consider corporate worship and church.

This is a big deal in families *and* in marriage. You should know what is expected concerning church attendance. Discuss how much time and effort you'll devote to working in the ministry and small group studies. A miscommunication in this area can wreak havoc in a marriage! Within the same faith, there are many different denominations; so again, you want to make sure you're both on the same page.

What are the marital expectations?

You both need to talk about the roles that each of you will play as a husband and a wife. Do you believe that a husband should be the head of the family? Are you willing to submit to your husband as the spiritual head of your household? Who do you think should do the chores? Who should pay the bills? Many marriages happen without *any* of these conversations taking place! What are your sexual expectations? Almost 50 percent of the divorces that happen are due to a miscommunication about sex, so this is an extremely important conversation to have! You shouldn't be engaging in sex before marriage, but you should be talking about it. Do you both want children? You would be surprised at the number of couples who marry without ever discussing this very important matter. Disagreement on whether or not you will have children can quickly drive a wedge between a husband and wife. Many women get blindsided without establishing these expectations, and

> "Almost 50 percent of the divorces that happen are due to a miscommunication about sex."

the marriage falls apart.

If you are going to move the next level in your relationship, and towards that expected end, you really should discuss these things. *Know* who your mate is *before* you start looking for the ring! Agreement is essential, and this is why you need to have these conversations before you consider the ring. Even if you have to agree to disagree and go your separate ways, there is no bitterness involved because you've agreed to your truths. Above all else, you don't want to get your heart invested in a man only to eventually find out that he isn't your ideal mate and your God-ordained husband.

Before you consider the ring, consider these things first!

CHAPTER 12

More Points to Discuss When Considering the Ring

"Do not conform to the pattern of this world, but be transformed by the renewing of your mind. Then you will be able to test and approve what God's." Romans 12:2

In the previous chapter, we touched on conversations that should be taking place *before* you consider the ring. We'll go a bit deeper into the matter with this chapter as well. Before you get married, you should *always* get pre-marital counseling so that you can determine if you and your mate are on the same page on various important aspects of marriage. You can choose to marry without the pre-marital

103

counseling if you like, but enter into the marriage at your own risk! The last thing you want is to get your heart attached to someone and then find out that you have differing viewpoints in crucial areas. Each of you should know where the other stands well in advance.

Consider your stances on children!

> ## "Before you get married, you should always get pre-marital counseling."

First and foremost, you need to discuss if both of you even *want* children! You should also discuss how you will raise children. Will you be expected to stay home and raise the children as a wife, or should there be some other arrangement? Will they be home-schooled entirely, or until they reach a certain age? There's also the matter of who will discipline the children, and how. You also have to consider your standpoints on different genders. How long do you allow your husband to nurture your daughter, and how long does he allow you to nurture your son?

How do you handle conflict?

"As sure as God sits on the throne, you will face conflict in your marriage!" It's impossible to live with your spouse *without* having conflict. As sure as God sits on the throne, you will face conflict in your marriage! Sometimes conflict can be a good thing, because it allows you to see how your significant other handles disagreement. How do they handle themselves under pressure? Are they angry, explosive, or abusive? These are things you *need* to know **before** you get the ring.

Consider finances and work!

Over 50 percent of marriages that end do so due to disagreements over finances. Finances can be a major pitfall in marriage. You have to talk about your finances before you ever talk about the ring. Who will be the breadwinner in the household? Most men may not want to admit it, but it sometimes makes them feel like less of a man if their wife makes more money! Does he expect you to stop working and take care of the kids, or continue to work and bring in extra income? If he expects you to take care of the kids, is it indefinitely, or until they are of school age? We talked about submission, but are you willing to submit financially as well? What happens if he wants you to end your career, or to put it on hold? This is a tough discussion to have, but it *must* be done.

> **"You have to talk about your finances before you ever talk about the ring."**

Consider how you handle on friendships!

Sometimes people may portray themselves as friends. The reality is that they are anything *but*! People say that misery loves company. We believe that misery is a spirit. People themselves may be miserable, but they'll drag you into their misery without that intention. Your friend is holding a pity party, and you're invited! A bigger consideration to make is how you will handle friends of the opposite sex, and your spouses' interaction with them. Do you trust your spouse alone with friends of the opposite sex, and will your spouse trust you? Will they even

> **"How you will handle friends of the opposite sex?"**

allow you to have friends of the opposite sex?

Again, these are tough conversations to have. However, these aren't meant to be easy. Another thing worth mentioning is that, getting what you believe to be the right answers to all of these considerations doesn't mean that you should let your guard down. Some people have the gift of the gab, and know all the right things to say. They know *everything* you want to hear. During your courtship and long before you ever begin down the road leading to marriage, be sure to have these discussions!

CHAPTER 13

How to Tell If You Are Ready

"Let each of you look not only to his own interests, but also to the interests of others."
Philippians 2:4 (ESV)

Your *Season of Singleness* is a blessing, not a curse. In fact, the sad thing is that many single ladies don't realize what a blessing this season is. It is in this season that you are free of the distractions that come along with marriage and family. You can focus solely on God and allow Him to show you your purpose, and His plan for you. If you allow it, God can prepare you to be the wife that your future husband needs. Just as He is preparing you to be a wife, He is also preparing your significant other to be your husband. It's imperative that you allow God to do the work that needs to be done. Remember, your *Season of Singleness* is about preparation *and* restoration.

> **"Your *Season of Singleness* is a blessing, not a curse."**

Single ladies may say that they're ready for marriage, but are you *really* ready?

> **"You get spat out, and wonder why you were left alone...again."**

Have you ever tried to cook a dish, and have it come out looking perfect only to find out that it wasn't quite done yet? The cake looked delicious and it smelled good, but it was still undone in the middle. The chicken might have looked golden brown on the outside, but was still red and bleeding when you took a bite. The same thing happens in relationships! You get into a relationship and say that you're ready for the ring, yet you are bleeding all over your significant other because you weren't ready. You get spat out, and wonder why you were left alone...again. It's all because you weren't ready for a relationship to begin with.

You may look in the mirror, and tell yourselves that you're ready, but when the true test comes, you fail miserably.

So how do you know if you're ready? Ask yourself these questions. When you do, look inwardly, and answer honestly.

Are you morally ready?

To answer that question, we'll go to the word of God, and look at Mark 7:20-23 which says, *"And He said, 'What comes out of a man, that defiles a man. For from within, out of the heart of men, proceed evil thoughts, adulteries, fornications, murders, thefts, covetousness, wickedness, deceit, lewdness, an evil eye, blasphemy, pride, foolishness. All these evil things come from within and defile a man.'"*

You say and do all the right things when others are around, but what's going on inside? It is what comes from within you that determines if you are ready. You above anyone else know that you have certain buttons, and if they are pressed, it will bring about what can defile you. The other person doesn't know that. Therefore, you have to ask yourself if you're morally ready, even if those buttons are pressed.

Are you emotionally stable?

"A fool vents all his feelings, but a wise **man** *holds them back." Proverbs 29:11*

To determine your emotional stability, you need only compare your emotional state to the scripture found in Proverbs 29:11. Do you feel as though you have to react to *everything* that someone else says or does to you? You have to make sure that you are not venting everything that you think. You must

> **"You should rule your emotions and not allow your emotions to rule over you."**

know how to bridle your emotions. You should rule your emotions and not allow your emotions to rule over you. If you respond to every criticism or offense with an outburst, you're not ready!

"Let love and faithfulness never leave you; bind them around your neck, write them on the tablet of your heart. Then you will win favor and a good name in the sight of God and man." Proverbs 3:3-4

A lot single ladies make the mistake of going out of their way to please the man in their lives in an effort to win his affections. They lower their standards and walk out of the will of God to please the man. In essence, they end up making the man their idol. Beloved, you don't ever make pleasing a man your priority. If you live a life that is pleasing in the eyes of the Father, then you will win favor in both God's sight, and in the sight of the man that He has prepared to be your husband! When you make pleasing God your greatest priority, and make Him your heart's desire, God will do the work within you that is necessary to places you in the position to be found. If you attempt to present yourself to a man before you are pleasing in God's eyes, God will reveal to that man that you're not ready! To the men that may be reading this, you need to seek a woman who loves God more than she love you!

> **"When you make pleasing God your greatest priority, and make Him your heart's desire."**

If you look at the story of Boaz and Ruth, it wasn't Ruth's outward appearance that attracted Boaz. She was out in the fields working, and her appearance wasn't that of beauty. What caught Boaz's attention was what radiated from the within her. Ruth never let love and faithfulness leave her. She wrote them on the tablet of her heart, and that is how she was able to find favor with God and with man. If your heart's desire is to please God, you will find favor. There's nothing wrong with wanting to have an extravagant wedding and a beautiful ring, but your main desire in this season should be to allow God to prepare you to be a wife.

Look back to Proverbs 18:22, which says, *"He who finds a wife finds a good thing, and obtains favor from the Lord."* This scripture is clear. You must already be a wife when your future husband arrives. If you are looking to be found by your Boaz, be ready. Look inward, and trust in God to prepare and restore you so that you may be a wife and be in position to be found.